AN
Epidemic
OF
Epigrams

—— *or* ——

An Avalanche of Aphorisms

DANIEL L. WICK

All rights reserved under International and Pan-American Copyright Conventions.
Published in the United States by Mirandola Press

Copyright © 2013 by Daniel L. Wick
All rights reserved.
ISBN: 1484051718
ISBN-13: 9781484051719

Library of Congress Control Number: 2013916252
CreateSpace Independent Publishing Platform, North Charleston, SC

To

Manfred Wolf, friend, mentor, and
aphorist extraordinaire.

And

Ben Holden, old friend and kind
but keen critic.

FOREWORD

The Epigram and the Aphorism

Epigrams are aphorisms and vice versa: brief, usually witty, occasionally profound observations on life, love, death, philosophy, religion, and virtually everything else.

Reading Oscar Wilde introduced me to the epigrammatic genre, which is why I prefer to use the term epigram. But everything I say here about epigrams also applies to aphorisms, except when I refer to authors as aphorists because although there is a word "epigrammatist," thankfully no one uses it.

The only distinction between the two that I have managed to uncover is that aphorisms are somewhat more pretentious epigrams.

As Manfred Wolf has observed in his brilliant essay *The Aphorism*, "Probably the greatest aphorist of all time was Shakespeare."[1] We need only pause for a moment to think of the hundreds of brief Shakespeare quotations that have become an essential part of the English language. Collections of aphorisms and epigrams almost always include dozens of contributions from Shakespeare.

---

[1] Manfred Wolf, "The Aphorism" ETC., Winter 1994-95, p. 432.

It is helpful to keep in mind that epigrams and aphorisms must stand on their own. As Dr. Johnson (no mean aphorist himself) observed, they are "unconnected" propositions. Or, as Manfred Wolf puts it, "an aphorism that requires a context is not an aphorism."[2]

I have arbitrarily placed epigrams under several subheadings, the philosophical, the witty, the paradox, the observational, the reverse cliché, the descriptive, the command, and the subversive.

An Example Of The Philosophical:

If God created us in his own image we have more than reciprocated.
-Voltaire

Of The Witty:

In married life three is company and two is none.
-Oscar Wilde

The Paradox:

By a curious confusion, many modern critics have passed from the proposition that a masterpiece may be unpopular to the other proposition that unless it is unpopular it cannot be a masterpiece.
- G. K. Chesterton

The Observational:

Soon you will have forgotten the world, and the world will have forgotten you.
- Marcus Aurelius

---

[2] Manfred Wolf, **Almost a Foreign Country ; A Personal Geography in Columns and Aphorisms** (2008), p. xviii. See Also John Gross, **The Oxford Book of Aphorisms** (2003), p. vii.

The Reverse Cliché:

Out of the mouths of babes comes drool.
— *Stanislaw Lec*

The Descriptive:

He is as great a fool who laughs at all as he that weeps at all.
— *Gracian*

The Command:

Resist not evil.
— *Jesus of Nazareth*

The Subversive:

When people do not respect us we are sharply offended; yet deep down in his heart no man much respects himself.
— *Mark Twain*

Indeed, all epigrams should to some extent be subversive. Their authors' intent is to compel or cajole the reader into reassessing conventional wisdom.

For example, as G.K. Chesterton pointed out in **The Everlasting Man**, Jesus was perhaps the most subversive of aphorists. Even two thousand years later, his pithy sayings retain their capacity to surprise and shock:[3]

Rejoice when reproached.

Bless those who curse you.

If struck on the cheek, offer the other.

---

[3] Burton L. Mack, **The Lost Gospel: the Book of Q and Christian Origins** (1993), pp. 110-12. Mack's translation.

Everyone who asks receives.

Give to everyone who begs.

Leave the dead to bury the dead.

Of course Jesus spoke often in parables. It is fair to say, paraphrasing Manfred Wolf, that Jesus' aphorisms are condensed parables just as his parables are expanded aphorisms.

Unfortunately, not all epigrams are either witty or wise. Many are trivial and tasteless. But even the worst require the reader to see things somewhat differently, if only for the moment.

The following represent an array of excellent epigrams:

The difference between stupidity and genius is that genius has its limits.
                                                                                    - Albert Einstein

Conversation is ultimately an attempt at overcoming isolation. Unfortunately, it often increases it.
                                                                                    - Manfred Wolf

Even if you're on the right track, you'll get run over if you just sit there.
                                                                                    - Will Rogers

Patriotism is supporting your country all the time, and your government when it deserves it.
                                                                                    - Mark Twain

It's called the "American Dream" because you have to be asleep to believe it.
                                                                                    - George Carlin

Comedy is merely tragedy happening to someone else.
                                                                                    - W. C. Fields

Men always want to be a woman's first love; women like to be a man's last romance.

- Oscar Wilde

Those who can make you believe absurdities can make you commit atrocities.

- Voltaire

I offer this collection of epigrams at one per page, not because I think they are especially important or equal in value but to encourage readers to browse at their leisure. In short, this is not a book intended to be read from beginning to end like a novel but rather sampled from time to time. I have also chosen to present them randomly, not chronologically as I wrote them or thematic, or arranged by the categories I have outlined in this **Foreword**. Through the unpredictability of the random, I hope to encourage readers constantly to shift mental gears.

DLW
July 2013

The sleek shall inherit the earth.

Small lies almost always conceal large truths.

The Bible begins with punishment for seeking knowledge and ends with sacrifice for finding faith. In between are several hundred pages of murder, slavery, and seduction that add to the plot but detract from the moral.

Love thy neighbor as thy mother-in-law.

Beauty is only sin deep.

Jesus had a problem with the truth. He told it.

Philology recapitulates ontology.

*History never repeats itself,
although sometimes
it stutters.*

*He never met a mirror
he didn't like.*

It is better to have loved and lost than never to have had cancer.

Success is a series of setbacks overcome.

*A legend is a lie that
tells the truth.*

A terrorist thinks locally and acts globally.

The mentally ill: Out of mind, out of sight.

The socialist credo: Let's be calm, cool, and collective.

It is the least I can do and I always strive to do the very least.

Wit is a brevity of soul.

There is many a cup 'twixt the lip and the slip.

He can actually tell the truth with a straight face.

Art represents but is never representative.

The bourgeoisie are the washed un-great.

———

In vino, vomit.

*Misogyny rarely results
in progeny.*

―――――――

Familiarity breeds.

Philanthropy refutes misanthropy.

If you see a blind beggar kick him. Why should you be kinder than God?

It is easier for a camel to go through the eye of a needle than it is to reform Wall Street.

Breasts spring eternal in the human hope.

Wit is the highest form of sarcasm.

*Too much is made of words,
and too little.*

The way to a man's heart is through his ego.

The unexamined life is the only life worth living.

———

Pain is the price you pay for getting old enough to feel it.

Most of life is trying to get comfortable and never succeeding.

We are as good as we are compelled to be and never as bad as we would like.

A church is a place where we consistently fail to worship the divine.

A friend in need is a distant acquaintance.

Praise is usually foolish and always welcome.

Political fanaticism occurs almost solely among the illiterati.

Definitions by definition cannot be true.

He is as honest as the day is long - but the days are getting shorter.

I enjoy privacy even from myself.

History may be one damned thing after another but it isn't the same damned thing.

Controlling people are rarely under control.

Why is there a word for thoughtless but not a word for thoughtmore?

Maxims are for Germans with guns.

Everything unimportant has already been said.

Essays are trying.

Ennui is catching.

Life is often dreamed but rarely lived.

No news is actually not news.

History is never wrong but historians are seldom right.

Power corrupts. Absolute power is great fun. Just ask God.

You shouldn't judge a cover by its book.

*The rule proves the exception.
All exceptions are rules.*

Two heads are better than none.

Every solution has its problem.

*It is a good wind that
blows no ill.*

―

Only in sex and politics can you have it both ways.

Women are from Venus; men are from Mecca.

———

Purgatory: the minimum wage of sin.

Why is it always darkest just before you turn on the light?

*Advice to the debt-ridden:
Live free or buy.*

Note to physicists: Avoid split infinities.

*I have the cowardice of
my convictions.*

———

The righteous are seldom right.

*Psychopaths will **always** hurt a fly.*

Note to torture victims: It is never too early to give up.

The price of freedom always goes up.

Chivalry is not dead, just dozing.

Life is pointless. That's the point.

He looks like he's back from the living.

*Be it ever so humble there's
no place like hell.*

Ask me no questions and I will tell you nothing.

A bird in the hand makes blowing the nose difficult.

He has both feet planted firmly in the air.

About his work habits I can safely say that he soaks the candle at both ends.

*The saintly regularly commit
spiritual seppuku.*

As babies know, all good things come to those who wail.

I will clean your clock if you promise not to beat me up.

She is the skim of the crop.

Don't cut off your face to spite your nose.

The quality of mendacity is not strained.

Beauty is in the eye of the beholden.

Choosers can't be beggars.

Better the Devil you know than the Devil with whom you are slightly acquainted.

He bores me to laughter.

When all is said and done, everything has been said and nothing has been done.

Fortune favors the grave.

You can't squeeze blood out of a turncoat.

He casts a short shadow.

Don't go there. Just go.

The early bird gets the germ.

He is a beard-faced liar.

*If thine eye offends thee
switch to the other eye.*

I don't even agree with myself all the time.

―――――◆―――――

*When God smiles Fate
plays tricks.*

Silence is silver.

*Mothers are the invention
of necessity.*

Axioms speak louder than aphorisms.

Revisionists are not necessarily right; they are merely more recent.

He wears his learning heavily.

Death is a debt all must pay.

Let sleeping dogs tell the truth.

Great minds do not think alike; they just think.

In physics understanding cause and effect is often problematic; in history understanding either is impossible.

It is jamais vu all over again.

———

He took it like a boy.

That's for you to know and me to find out.

Our bodies, our graves.

Money talks; loyalty whispers.

Only *the means justify the ends.*

*If you can't stand the kitchen
get out of the heat.*

Beauty is trash and trash beauty. That is all ye postmodernists know and want to know.

Platitudes do not respect latitudes.

Atheists and dyslexics agree: they have no god in this fight.

*Rumors are wishes
unfulfilled.*

*Moderns communicate
almost entirely by cliché.*

Nice guys never finish.

Opposites retract.

Where there is smoke there is often a smoke machine.

Don't let thy left hand know what thy left hand is doing.

He's always grasping at flaws.

Organized religion is an inferior substitute for religion.

The wages of sin should be raised.

Early to bed and early to rise makes you very, very old.

An apple a day artificially keeps up the price of apples.

A penny saved is bad for business.

Waste not, want everything.

Give or it will be taken from you.

If thy right hand offend thee, wash it with thy left hand.

Even when we get things right we ultimately get them wrong.

He is the smartest man in the room only when he is alone.

———

There is more to you than meets the I.

Shepherds excel in thinking outside the flocks.

There are more effects than causes.

Many are called but few are awake.

The devil is in retail.

When in Rome do as the Greeks do.

Sin in haste, repeat at leisure.

Life is largely learning how to breathe.

*Money doesn't grow
on fees.*

———

The more we learn the less we know.

A rising tide drowns us all.

*The owl of Minerva
never flies.*

For every action there is an equal and opposite reactionary.

*Thinking well is the
best revenge.*

Don't place too many ironies in the fire.

You can't legislate immorality.

All talk is small talk.

It is time to shuffle off this moral coil.

All's well that ends.